To

_____

We love because he first loved us.
1 John 4:19

From

_____

Couples' Devotional Bible
Copyright © 1995 by Zondervan Corporation
All rights reserved

ISBN: 0-310-96243-9

Excerpts taken from:

Couples' Devotional Bible: New International Version® 1994 by Zondervan Publishing House.
The Holy Bible: New International Version® Copyright © 1973, 1978, 1984, by International
Bible Society. Used by permission of Zondervan Publishing House. All rights reserved.

The "NIV" and "New International Version" trademarks are registered in the United States
Patent and Trademark office by International Bible Society.

Requests for information should be addressed to:

ZondervanPublishingHouse
Grand Rapids, Michigan 49530

Project Editor: Leslie Berg Hoffman

Printed in China

96 97 98 / HK/ 5 4 3

January 1

So God created man in his own image, in the image of God he created him; male and female he created them.

Genesis 1:27

You are probably well aware of your differences. But what are some of the ways you are similar? How have your differences and similarities strengthened your marriage?

December 31

Therefore we do not lose heart. Though outwardly we are wasting away, yet inwardly we are being renewed day by day. For our light and momentary troubles are achieving for us an eternal glory that far outweighs them all.

2 Corinthians 4:16-17

How have you experienced God's grace in moments of sorrow or trouble in your family?

January 2

The LORD God said, "It is not good for the man to be alone.
I will make a helper suitable for him."

Genesis 2:18

Has there been a time when you put one of your individual
dreams "on hold" so your spouse could pursue a dream?
Was the eventual outcome positive for both of you?

December 30

For the Lamb at the center of the throne will be their shepherd;
he will lead them to springs of living water. And God will wipe
away every tear from their eyes.

Revelation 7:17

Why is it so hard not to "borrow trouble"
from tomorrow by worrying?

January 3

For this reason a man will leave his father and mother and be united to his wife, and they will become one flesh.

Genesis 2:24

How has God "blended" you to maximize your usefulness for his kingdom? How can you both be more open to his blending?

December 29

Moreover, we have all had human fathers who disciplined us and we respected them for it. How much more should we submit to the Father of our spirits and live! Our fathers disciplined us for a little while as they thought best; but God disciplines us for our good, that we may share in his holiness.

Hebrews 12:9-10

What practical things can you do to avoid the two extremes that lead a child to "rebellion" or "chaos"?

January 4

*But Abel brought fat portions from some of the firstborn of his flock.
The LORD looked with favor on Abel and his offering.*

Genesis 4:4

How satisfied are you with your present level of charitable giving?
How can you make giving a higher priority each month? Each year?

December 28

Those whom I love I rebuke and discipline. So be earnest, and repent.

Revelation 3:19

How does a loving relationship with your child
provide a balance for your attempts to discipline him or her?

January 5

*Noah was a righteous man, blameless among the people
of his time, and he walked with God.*

Genesis 6:9

In what ways do you reach out for fellowship with God?

December 27

To him who is able to keep you from falling and to present you before his glorious presence without fault and with great joy—to the only God our Savior be glory, majesty, power and authority, through Jesus Christ our Lord, before all ages, now and forevermore! Amen.

Jude 24-25

In what areas does perfectionism creep into your goals for your marriage and your family? How can you relax and depend on God's presence as a third partner in your marriage team?

January 6

Noah found favor in the eyes of the LORD.
Genesis 6:8

How would you characterize your "walk" with God—
comfortable, close, distanced, awkward? What might make
walking with God a more natural habit for you?

December 26

Dear friend, do not imitate what is evil but what is good. Anyone who does what is good is from God. Anyone who does what is evil has not seen God.

3 John 11

What loving behaviors have become more natural over the years of your marriage? Are you doing all you can to express your love in ways your spouse can recognize?

January 7

When Jacob awoke from his sleep, he thought, "Surely the LORD is in this place, and I was not aware of it."

Genesis 28:16

Why is it that a sense of God's nearness is so difficult to keep foremost in our minds? What steps can you take to remind yourself to rejoice in God's presence all day long—as individuals, as a couple and as a family?

December 25

Do not conform any longer to the pattern of this world, but be transformed by the renewing of your mind. Then you will be able to test and approve what God's will is—his good, pleasing and perfect will.

Romans 12:2

What do you do to refresh your mind when impure or unwholesome thoughts seem to get stuck there?

January 8

And now, do not be distressed and do not be angry with yourselves for selling me here, because it was to save lives that God sent me ahead of you.

Genesis 45:5

How has forgiveness been constructive in your own marriage? What issues in your relationship might be resolved through forgiveness?

December 24

If anyone comes to you and does not bring this teaching,
do not take him into your house or welcome him.

2 John 10

In what practical ways could God's standards
help you in monitoring what comes into your home
via television or other media?

January 9

*All these are the twelve tribes of Israel, and this is what
their father said to them when he blessed them, giving
each the blessing appropriate to him.*

Genesis 49:28

How do the blessings of touch and verbal encouragement
come into play in your family?

December 23

This is the confidence we have in approaching God: that if we ask anything according to his will, he hears us. And if we know that he hears us—whatever we ask—we know that we have what we asked of him.

1 John 5:14-15

When has God answered your prayers in ways you could never have anticipated? Do you believe that all resources are at God's disposal? How does that affect your family's financial planning?

January 10

Then Jacob called for his sons and said: "Gather around so I can tell you what will happen to you in days to come."

Genesis 49:1

How can you help your children see that they have a special future—here on earth, and later in heaven with God?

December 22

Whoever does not love does not know God, because God is love.
1 John 4:8

How would you describe the love you have for your spouse?
Share with each other examples of married couples who
have modeled love for you. What lessons from
their love could you learn to apply to your own marriage?

January 11

So now, go. I am sending you to Pharaoh to bring my people the Israelites out of Egypt.

Exodus 3:10

When has your relationship with God encountered a "desert" period? How did you respond in that situation? What positive consequences can you identify as a result of going through a dry or difficult time in your marriage?

December 21

Dear children, let us not love with words or tongue but with actions and in truth.

1 John 3:18

In what ways have you lived out 1 John 3:18 before your spouse?

January 12

You shall not commit adultery.

Exodus 20:14

What effects has adultery had on the
marriages of people you know?

December 20

Be devoted to one another in brotherly love.
Honor one another above yourselves.

Romans 12:10

What do you think are the essential factors that
hold today's marriages together?

January 13

My son, keep my words and store up my commands within you. . . .
Bind them on your fingers; write them on the tablet of your heart.
Proverbs 7:1,3

What practical steps can you take to "affair-proof" your marriage?

December 19

The Lord is not slow in keeping his promise, as some understand slowness. He is patient with you, not wanting anyone to perish, but everyone to come to repentance.

2 Peter 3:9

In what ways can you pattern your marriage relationship after God's loving acceptance?

January 14

For six years you are to sow your fields and harvest the crops, but during the seventh year let the land lie unplowed and unused. Then the poor among your people may get food from it, and the wild animals may eat what they leave. Do the same with your vineyard and your olive grove.

Exodus 23:10-11

What adjustments can you make in your weekly schedule to have regular time with your spouse? What benefits to your marriage might come from adhering to a regular "fallow" time together?

December 18

A man's wisdom gives him patience;
it is to his glory to overlook an offense.
Proverbs 19:11

How patient are you when you have to wait for
your spouse to learn something?

January 15

The LORD replied, "My Presence will go with you,
and I will give you rest."

Exodus 33:14

How would you characterize your lifestyle?

December 17

For this very reason, make every effort to add to your faith goodness; and to goodness, knowledge; and to knowledge, self-control; and to self-control, perseverance; and to perseverance, godliness; and to godliness, brotherly kindness; and to brotherly kindness, love.

2 Peter 1:5-7

Privately think back over your own interaction with your spouse over the last 24 hours. In what ways could you have offered more courtesy or encouragement?

January 16

This is what the Sovereign LORD, the Holy One of Israel,
says: "In repentance and rest is your salvation, in quietness
and trust is your strength."

Isaiah 30:15

What changes—even drastic ones—might be necessary to
maintain your priorities as a spouse and parent?

December 16

Humble yourselves, therefore, under God's mighty hand,
that he may lift you up in due time.

1 Peter 5:6

Why does receiving God's good gifts make you feel humble before him? What are some of God's greatest gifts to you?

January 17

I am the LORD *your God; consecrate yourselves and be holy, because I am holy. Do not make yourselves unclean by any creature that moves about on the ground.*

Leviticus 11:44

How has your relationship with God changed you? How has being married to your spouse made you a better person?

December 15

Above all, love each other deeply, because love
covers over a multitude of sins.

1 Peter 4:8

What are some ways your spouse shows that he or
she loves you? How can you appreciate your spouse's "romance
language," even when it is different from your own?

January 18

Do not seek revenge or bear a grudge against one of your people,
but love your neighbor as yourself. I am the LORD.

Leviticus 19:18

What are some ways you quietly "get even" when
your spouse hurts you? How can you handle
the hurt more constructively?

December 14

A new command I give you: Love one another. As I have loved you, so you must love one another. By this all men will know that you are my disciples, if you love one another.

John 13:34-35

How can you shift your perspective from trying to change your mate to working on areas where you personally need to change?

January 19

*A tithe of everything from the land, whether grain from the soil or fruit from the trees, belongs to the L*ORD*; it is holy to the L*ORD.

Leviticus 27:30

How would you characterize your giving "attitude"? What steps can the two of you take to change any attitudes that are not characterized by "cheerful giving"?

December 13

*Wives, in the same way be submissive to your husbands so that,
if any of them do not believe the word, they may be won over without
words by the behavior of their wives.*

1 Peter 3:1

Can you pinpoint a recent time when having
spent time with God improved your marriage relationship?
What effect did it have?

January 20

The LORD is slow to anger, abounding in love and forgiving sin and rebellion. Yet he does not leave the guilty unpunished; he punishes the children for the sin of the fathers to the third and fourth generation.

Numbers 14:18

How have you exhibited patience in your marriage over the past week? Where do you need more patience?

December 12

*Instead, speaking the truth in love, we will in all things
grow up into him who is the Head, that is, Christ. From him the
whole body, joined and held together by every supporting ligament,
grows and builds itself up in love, as each part does its work.*

Ephesians 4:15-16

How is your love for one another evidence of your spiritual life?

January 21

Bear with each other and forgive whatever grievances you may have against one another. Forgive as the Lord forgave you.

Colossians 3:13

How does God's patience in dealing with you help you as you are patient with others?

December 11

Like newborn babies, crave pure spiritual milk,
so that by it you may grow up in your salvation.
1 Peter 2:2

In what ways do you think you personally have
"grown up" since you were married?

January 22

When a man makes a vow to the LORD or takes an oath to obligate himself by a pledge, he must not break his word but must do everything he said.

Numbers 30:2

What problems or enticements might tempt you to break your marriage vows?

December 10

These have come so that your faith—of greater worth than gold, which perishes even though refined by fire—may be proved genuine and may result in praise, glory and honor when Jesus Christ is revealed.

1 Peter 1:7

What are three ways in which your spouse thinks and responds differently than you do? How do you deal with each of these differences in order to live harmoniously together?

January 23

Therefore what God has joined together, let man not separate.
Mark 10:9

Affirm to your spouse your commitment to remain together
"for as long as you both shall live."

December 9

Therefore confess your sins to each other and pray for each other so that you may be healed. The prayer of a righteous man is powerful and effective.

James 5:16

In what ways have you found prayer to be the "cement" that holds your marriage together? If there is any area of conflict between the two of you right now, stop and take time to pray about it together.

January 24

*But commission Joshua, and encourage and strengthen him,
for he will lead this people across and will cause them to
inherit the land that you will see.*

Deuteronomy 3:28

What challenges is your spouse facing for which your
encouragement would provide a boost? What are two practical
things you can do this week to encourage your spouse?

December 8

Search me, O God, and know my heart;
test me and know my anxious thoughts.

Psalm 139:23

What satisfaction do you find in knowing that God
knows and understands you completely?

January 25

For the LORD your God is a consuming fire, a jealous God.

Deuteronomy 4:24

How have you learned to fit times of prayer and focusing on God into spare moments of your day? What are regular times of prayer you share as a couple?

December 7

Come near to God and he will come near to you. Wash your hands, you sinners, and purify your hearts, you double-minded.

James 4:8

How is fully understanding each other harder than you may have thought before you were married?

January 26

*These commandments that I give you today are to be upon
your hearts. Impress them on your children. Talk about them
when you sit at home and when you walk along the road,
when you lie down and when you get up.*

Deuteronomy 6:6-7

What does your marriage teach to children who see it up close?

December 6

Who is wise and understanding among you? Let him show it
by his good life, by deeds done in the humility that comes from wisdom.
But if you harbor bitter envy and selfish ambition in your hearts,
do not boast about it or deny the truth.

James 3:13-14

What aspects of your relationship make you feel close to,
or intimate with, your spouse? On your own, consider additional
ways you might serve your spouse today.

January 27

*Don't let anyone look down on you because you are young,
but set an example for the believers in speech, in life,
in love, in faith and in purity.*

· 1 Timothy 4:12

Whose marriage has served as a good
example for you as a couple? Why?

December 5

Perseverance must finish its work so that you may be mature and complete, not lacking anything.

James 1:4

Identify and describe a time when you tried a "quick" solution for an ongoing problem in your marriage. What happened? What are some other areas where patience comes into play in your relationship with each other?

January 28

Know then in your heart that as a man disciplines his son,
so the LORD your God disciplines you.

Deuteronomy 8:5

How, specifically, do you lovingly demand obedience
from your children? Identify the goals of godly behavior in your
family. What practical changes could you make in your discipline
style that would help your family reach those goals?

December 4

The eyes of all look to you, and you give them their food at the proper time. You open your hand and satisfy the desires of every living thing. The LORD is righteous in all his ways and loving toward all he has made.

Psalm 145:15-17

When was it hardest for you to trust God during
a difficult period of your life?

January 29

Fix these words of mine in your hearts and minds; tie them as symbols on your hands and bind them on your foreheads. Teach them to your children, talking about them when you sit at home and when you walk along the road, when you lie down and when you get up.

Deuteronomy 11:18-19

Who are the people, starting with yourself, who are affected by the way you live your life for God?

December 3

*No discipline seems pleasant at the time, but painful.
Later on, however, it produces a harvest of righteousness and
peace for those who have been trained by it.*

Hebrews 12:11

When was the last time you felt that God was "pruning"
something out of your life? What was the outcome?

January 30

Fathers, do not exasperate your children; instead, bring them up in the training and instruction of the Lord.

Ephesians 6:4

What truths and values do you hope your children will "catch" from you?

December 2

*Now faith is being sure of what we hope for and
certain of what we do not see.*

Hebrews 11:1

What are the advantages of two people trusting the Lord together?
How does God's peace offset up and down times?

January 31

Have I not commanded you? Be strong and courageous.
Do not be terrified; do not be discouraged, for the LORD your
God will be with you wherever you go.

Joshua 1:9

When have you gone ahead with something you knew was
right, despite your fears? What anxieties do you hold about
the future of your marriage, and how could your loving
obedience to God help you face those fears?

December 1

*And let us consider how we may spur one another on
toward love and good deeds. Let us not give up meeting together,
as some are in the habit of doing, but let us encourage one another—
and all the more as you see the Day approaching.*

Hebrews 10:24-25

How might you tell your partner "I believe in you"
without using those words? In what ways has your spouse
been an encouragement to you?

February 1

The LORD turned to him and said, "Go in the strength you have and save Israel out of Midian's hand. Am I not sending you?"
Judges 6:14

What task is before you that makes you feel inadequate?
How can you encourage each other to go forward in
obedience—with confidence?

November 30

*God is not unjust; he will not forget your work
and the love you have shown him as you have helped his
people and continue to help them.*

Hebrews 6:10

What is one area where you are weak but your spouse is strong?
An area where you are strong, but your spouse is not-so-strong?
Have you been able to help each other in these areas?

February 2

Again the Israelites did evil in the eyes of the LORD. They served
the Baals and the Ashtoreths, and the gods of Aram, the gods of Sidon,
the gods of Moab, the gods of the Ammonites and the gods of the
Philistines. And because the Israelites forsook the LORD and no
longer served him, he became angry with them.

Judges 10:6-7a

What has your mate done or said in the past few weeks
that really annoyed you? How can you communicate
patience and mercy in your actions?

November 29

For this reason he had to be made like his brothers in every way,
in order that he might become a merciful and faithful high priest in
service to God, and that he might make atonement for the sins
of the people. Because he himself suffered when he was tempted,
he is able to help those who are being tempted.

Hebrews 2:17-18

How does it help to know that, because Christ was a man,
God understands our longings and weaknesses?

February 3

But Ruth replied, "Don't urge me to leave you or to turn back
from you. Where you go I will go, and where you stay I will stay.
Your people will be my people and your God my God."

Ruth 1:16

What unsettling changes are you currently facing?

November 28

For we do not have a high priest who is unable to sympathize with our weaknesses, but we have one who has been tempted in every way, just as we are—yet was without sin.

Hebrews 4:15

How does a lack of forgiveness lead to loneliness in your relationship?

February 4

Forget the former things; do not dwell on the past. See, I am doing a new thing! Now it springs up; do you not perceive it? I am making a way in the desert and streams in the wasteland.

Isaiah 43:18-19

Despite the risks of change, how can you look forward
to new areas of growth?

November 27

I do wish, brother, that I may have some benefit from you in the Lord; refresh my heart in Christ.

Philemon 20

When have your personal anxieties or problems been eased because of your spouse's care and attention?

February 5

But be sure to fear the LORD and serve him faithfully with all your heart; consider what great things he has done for you.

1 Samuel 12:24

Does remembering God's goodness to you in the past affect your desire to serve him as a couple? How can you cultivate a habit of "counting your blessings"?

November 26

Your love has given me great joy and encouragement, because you, brother, have refreshed the hearts of the saints.

Philemon 7

How have you seen God's love in your spouse's caring acts?

February 6

But Samuel replied: "Does the LORD delight in burnt offerings and sacrifices as much as in obeying the voice of the LORD? To obey is better than sacrifice, and to heed is better than the fat of rams."

1 Samuel 15:22

What items would you like to pray about each day with each other? How might you create a time to pray together regularly?

November 25

He who listens to a life-giving rebuke will be at home among the wise.

Proverbs 15:31

How can you cultivate that "listening" ear and a
spirit that's open to change?

February 7

But the LORD said to Samuel, "Do not consider his appearance
or his height, for I have rejected him. The LORD does not look at the
things man looks at. Man looks at the outward appearance, but
the LORD looks at the heart."

1 Samuel 16:7

What is something you love about your spouse that you didn't
even know about him or her when you first got married?

November 24

These, then, are the things you should teach. Encourage and rebuke with all authority. Do not let anyone despise you.

Titus 2:15

Why is it easier to take criticism or a "rebuke" from someone who loves you—like a spouse or your children?

February 8

Your beauty should not come from outward adornment, such as braided hair and the wearing of gold jewelry and fine clothes. Instead, it should be that of your inner self, the unfading beauty of a gentle and quiet spirit, which is of great worth in God's sight.

1 Peter 3:3-4

What are some of the rewards of loving your *real* spouse instead of his or her image?

November 23

*You, however, know all about my teaching, my way of life, my purpose,
faith, patience, love, endurance, persecutions, sufferings—what kinds of
things happened to me in Antioch, Iconium and Lystra, the persecutions
I endured. Yet the Lord rescued me from all of them.*

2 Timothy 3:10-11

When have you experienced peace and confidence
in the face of difficulty?

February 9

*O Sovereign LORD, you are God! Your words are trustworthy,
and you have promised these good things to your servant. Now be
pleased to bless the house of your servant, that it may continue forever
in your sight; for you, O Sovereign LORD, have spoken, and with your
blessing the house of your servant will be blessed forever.*

2 Samuel 7:28-29

What specific prayer requests come to mind as you consider your
hopes and dreams for your family? How could you become more
bold and persistent in praying for God's blessing on your family?

November 22

But as for you, continue in what you have learned and have become convinced of, because you know those from who you learned it, and how from infancy you have known the holy Scriptures, which are able to make you wise for salvation through faith in Christ Jesus.

2 Timothy 3:14-15

How does studying God's Word regularly equip you for today and for the future?

February 10

As for God, his way is perfect; the word of the LORD is flawless.
He is a shield for all who take refuge in him.

2 Samuel 22:31

When do portions of Scripture from your personal Bible reading
or study resurface to influence your day-to-day life?

November 21

Flee the evil desires of youth, and pursue righteousness, faith, love and peace, along with those who call on the Lord out of a pure heart.

2 Timothy 2:22

What are some of the "hedges"—or personal standards—you've set for yourself to avoid temptations? Are there ways you can team up to fight temptation?

February 11

For the word of God is living and active. Sharper than any double-edged sword, it penetrates even to dividing soul and spirit, joints and marrow; it judges the thoughts and attitudes of the heart.

Hebrews 4:12

In what ways do you remind yourselves and each other of important truths from God's Word?

November 20

For God did not give us a spirit of timidity,
but a spirit of power, of love and of self-discipline.

2 Timothy 1:7

In what situations do you feel overwhelmed by negative
feelings? How do you exercise God's gift of a "spirit of power,
of love and of self-discipline?"

February 12

*Now, O L*ORD *my God, you have made your servant king in place of my father David. But I am only a little child and do not know how to carry out my duties. Your servant is here among the people you have chosen, a great people, too numerous to count or number. So give your servant a discerning heart to govern your people and to distinguish between right and wrong.*

1 Kings 3:7-9a

If you could improve any two areas of your marriage, what would they be? In what ways do you need to change to help bring about those improvements?

November 19

For the love of money is a root of all kinds of evil. Some people,
eager for money, have wandered from the faith and pierced
themselves with many griefs.

1 Timothy 6:10

How do "godliness" and "contentment" combine
to make the Christan's life rich?

February 13

But your hearts must be fully committed to the LORD our God, to live by his decrees and obey his commands, as at this time.

1 Kings 8:61

Recall a time when *feelings* failed you, and you loved because you had committed to love each other. How have others in your life shown the kind of love that is not swayed by circumstances or feelings?

November 18

But godliness with contentment is great gain.
1 Timothy 6:6

If "contentment is natural wealth," as once stated by Socrates,
how rich are you as a couple and as a family?

February 14

Remember, O Lord, how I have walked before you faithfully and with wholehearted devotion and have done what is good in your eyes.

2 Kings 20:3

What are the challenges you face as a Christian as you
try to be faithful to God?

November 17

But if a widow has children or grandchildren, these should learn first of all to put their religion into practice by caring for their own family and so repaying their parents and grandparents, for this is pleasing to God.

1 Timothy 5:4

Based on a list of activities that each of you makes time for on a regular basis, where does "couple time" rank in relation to the other involvements? What are the most common distractions that keep you from spending enough time together as a couple? What can you do this month to free up more time to do more things together?

February 15

But the fruit of the Spirit is love, joy, peace, patience, kindness, goodness, faithfulness, gentleness and self-control.

Galatians 5:22-23a

What challenges are part of faithfulness in marriage?

November 16

Be diligent in these matters; give yourself wholly to them, so that everyone may see your progress. Watch your life and doctrine closely. Persevere in them, because if you do, you will save both yourself and your hearers.

1 Timothy 4:15-16

How have you encouraged each other to put your God-given talents and gifts to work?

February 16

Josiah was eight years old when he became king, and he reigned in
Jerusalem thirty-one years. His mother's name was Jedidah daughter
of Adaiah; she was from Bozkath. He did what was right in the eyes
of the LORD and walked in all the ways of his father David,
not turning aside to the right or to the left.

2 Kings 22:1-2

What are some of your spouse's visible achievements?
Each of your children's? What are some of the less obvious
character traits you can affirm in them?

November 15

*Set an example for the believers in speech, in life, in love,
in faith and in purity. Until I come, devote yourself to the public
reading of Scripture, to preaching and to teaching. Do not neglect
your gift, which was given you through a prophetic message when
the body of elders laid their hands on you.*

1 Timothy 4:12b-14

How does your spouse's confidence in
you bolster your own courage?

February 17

Look to the LORD and his strength; seek his face always.

1 Chronicles 16:11

Apart from Sunday worship at church, how do you incorporate
personal times of worshiping God into your life?

November 14

However, each one of you also must love his wife as he loves himself, and the wife must respect her husband.

Ephesians 5:33

How would your older children grade your marriage?

February 18

For great is the LORD and most worthy of praise; he is to be feared above all gods. . . . Bring an offering and come before him; worship the LORD in the splendor of his holiness.

1 Chronicles 16:25,29b

Why does worship have an effect on your sinful behaviors?

November 13

A deacon must be the husband of but one wife and must manage his children and his household well. Those who have served well gain an excellent standing and great assurance in their faith in Christ Jesus.

1 Timothy 3:12-13

What things do your children seem to notice or learn from aspects of your relationship as a married couple?

February 19

*Then you will have success if you are careful to observe the decrees
and laws that the LORD gave Moses for Israel. Be strong and courageous.
Do not be afraid or discouraged.*

1 Chronicles 22:13

How has your love for each other, and for God, been deepened
as a result of persevering through past struggles in your marriage?
Which one of you needs the most help now, and how can
the other best provide the help that is needed?

November 12

For Adam was formed first, then Eve.

1 Timothy 2:13

In what areas have you and your spouse developed
interdependence? In what areas has your teamwork improved
since the early days of your marriage?

February 20

He said: O LORD, God of Israel, there is no God like you in heaven or on earth—you who keep your covenant of love with your servants who continue wholeheartedly in your way.

2 Chronicles 6:14

Describe the difference between a covenant and a contract. Why does a binding agreement like the marriage covenant actually provide a context of freedom for you and your spouse?

November 11

But for that very reason I was shown mercy so that in me, the worst of sinners, Christ Jesus might display his unlimited patience as an example for those who would believe on him and receive eternal life.

1 Timothy 1:16

How do you react to the contention that "ensured happiness" is one of the myths of marriage? What are you doing to make happiness a reality in your own marriage?

February 21

If my people, who are called by my name, will humble themselves and pray and seek my face and turn from their wicked ways, then will I hear from heaven and will forgive their sin and will heal their land.

2 Chronicles 7:14

Does each of you feel that the other supports you in prayer?
In what ways does that lighten your burdens?

November 10

May the Lord direct your hearts into God's love and Christ's perseverance.

2 Thessalonians 3:5

Do you feel your marriage is stronger today than it was a year ago? Why or why not? Double-check your marriage against each aspect of the fruit of the Spirit listed in Galatians 5:22-23. How does your life reflect these qualities?

February 22

I have chosen and consecrated this temple so that my Name may be there forever. My eyes and my heart will always be there.

2 Chronicles 7:16

When have you felt sure of God's presence as you prayed together? Have you recognized God's answers to those prayers?

November 9

May our Lord Jesus Christ himself and God our Father, who loved us and by his grace gave us eternal encouragement and good hope, encourage your hearts and strengthen you in every good deed and word.

2 Thessalonians 2:16-17

Name some areas where you and your spouse have opposite, but complementary, talents or gifts. When has it been hard for you to let go and really depend on your spouse?

February 23

*Now let the fear of the LORD be upon you. Judge carefully, for with the
LORD our God there is no injustice or partiality or bribery.*

2 Chronicles 19:7

Have you ever discovered that your perception of your
mate's attitudes or actions was inaccurate? What did you
learn from that experience?

November 8

With this in mind, we constantly pray for you, that our God may count you worthy of his calling, and that by his power he may fulfill every good purpose of yours and every act prompted by your faith.

2 Thessalonians 1:11

How can praying for your spouse help insure that God's work will be done in his or her life, and not your own work? Write down three things your spouse would like you to be praying for this week.

February 24

Consider carefully what you do, because you are not judging for man but for the LORD, who is with you whenever you give a verdict.

2 Chronicles 19:6

Though we cannot be omniscient, as God is, how can you employ wisdom in your discernment about others?

November 7

*Give thanks in all circumstances, for this is God's
will for you in Christ Jesus.*

1 Thessalonians 5:18

In past times of disappointment or depression, what restored
you to stability and joy? Sometimes writing things down makes
them more tangible or memorable to us. Consider keeping a daily
journal of things you want to thank God for.

February 25

Also in Judah the hand of God was on the people to give them unity of mind to carry out what the king and his officials had ordered, following the word of the LORD.

2 Chronicles 30:12

How have you handled it when one of you began to feel God calling you to some change in your lives? As God has blended you as a couple, how have each of you improved as individuals?

November 6

For God did not call us to be impure, but to live a holy life.
Therefore, he who rejects this instruction does not reject man but God,
who gives you his Holy Spirit.

1 Thessalonians 4:7-8

What are ways you could help each other avoid sexually explicit
images that sometimes lead to impure thoughts?

February 26

*So we fasted and petitioned our God about this,
and he answered our prayer.*

Ezra 8:23

When do you most worry about your spouse's and your children's
physical well-being? How could those times serve as a good
reminder to pray for their spiritual safety?

November 5

It is God's will . . . that each of you should learn to control his own body in a way that is holy and honorable, not in passionate lust like the heathen, who do not know God.

1 Thessalonians 4:3a,4-5

How do you strive to maintain purity in your own thought life?

February 27

Then I said: O LORD, God of heaven, the great and awesome God,
who keeps his covenant of love with those who love him and obey his
commands, let your ear be attentive and your eyes open to hear the prayer
your servant is praying before you day and night for your servants,
the people of Israel. I confess the sins we Israelites, including myself
and my father's house, have committed against you.

Nehemiah 1:5-6

What fears keep you from sharing openly with your spouse?

November 4

But, brothers, when we were torn away from you for a
short time (in person, not in thought), out of our intense longing
we made every effort to see you.

1 Thessalonians 2:17

How do you update each other on your individual lives—whether
you're traveling or at home together? What specific things could
each of you do to better involve each other in your individual lives?

February 28

O Lord, let your ear be attentive to the prayer of this your servant and to the prayer of your servants who delight in revering your name.

Nehemiah 1:11a

What fears keep you from feeling free to approach God in prayer?

November 3

*Let your conversation be always full of grace, seasoned with salt,
so that you may know how to answer everyone.*

Colossians 4:6

When have you found yourselves speaking two different
languages when trying to communicate about something?
How do you communicate your love to your spouse?
How clearly does your message get through?

February 29

*They refused to listen and failed to remember the miracles you
performed among them. They became stiff-necked and in their rebellion
appointed a leader in order to return to their slavery. But you
are a forgiving God, gracious and compassionate, slow to anger and
abounding in love. Therefore you did not desert them.*

Nehemiah 9:17

On a day-to-day basis, you probably forgive many minor
things without ever discussing the forgiveness. What are the
more major areas that you feel forgiveness needs to be
asked for, and communicated?

November 2

Do not let any unwholesome talk come out of your mouths, but only what is helpful for building others up according to their needs, that it may benefit those who listen.

Ephesians 4:29

How is acceptance communicated in words
and actions at your house?

March 1

For if you forgive men when they sin against you, your heavenly Father will also forgive you. But if you do not forgive men their sins, your Father will not forgive your sins.

Matthew 6:14-15

How does forgiving free you to let go of the past
and look ahead to the future?

November 1

Fathers, do not embitter your children,
or they will become discouraged.
Colossians 3:21

Describe a time when another
person's criticisms made you feel defeated.

March 2

And as they were drinking wine on that second day, the king again asked, "Queen Esther, what is your petition? It will be given you. What is your request? Even up to half the kingdom, it will be granted."

Esther 7:2

Have you ever gotten something you wanted from your spouse by using manipulative tactics? How can you respect your spouse at the same time you communicate what you need and want?

October 31

And we pray this in order that you may live a life worthy of the Lord and may please him in every way: bearing fruit in every good work, growing in the knowledge of God.

Colossians 1:10

What are the benefits of growing together, despite your differences? In what ways has accepting and accommodating each other become an ongoing part of your marriage?

March 3

At this, Job got up and tore his robe and shaved his head. Then he fell to the ground in worship and said: "Naked I came from my mother's womb, and naked I will depart. The LORD gave and the LORD has taken away; may the name of the LORD be praised."

Job 1:20-21

What are some of the struggles and losses you've experienced during the years of your marriage? How were you able to love and trust God, despite these painful experiences?

October 30

I know what it is to be in need, and I know what it is to have plenty.
I have learned the secret of being content in any and every situation,
whether well fed or hungry, whether living in plenty or in want.
I can do everything through him who gives me strength.

Philippians 4:12-13

Are certain circumstances robbing you of the peace and joy
that are part of contentment? Take time today to remind each
other of God's loving intentions for you and your life.

March 4

Blessed is the man whom God corrects; so do not despise the discipline of the Almighty.

Job 5:17

What are some of the limits children need but are unable to ask for themselves? Why is a home atmosphere of loving acceptance so crucial for preventing a young person from latching onto destructive habits?

October 29

*I am not saying this because I am in need, for I have learned
to be content whatever the circumstances.*

Philippians 4:11

In what areas of your life do you tend to be "self-sufficient"?

March 5

Though he slay me, yet will I hope in him;
I will surely defend my ways to his face.

Job 13:15

How have you worked through a time of spiritual doubting,
a time when you questioned God's love, or goodness or
presence? Who might provide much-needed support
if you encounter such a time in the future?

October 28

What is more, I consider everything a loss compared to the surpassing greatness of knowing Christ Jesus my Lord, for whose sake I have lost all things. I consider them rubbish, that I may gain Christ.

Philippians 3:8

What have you had to lose or let go of in order to keep your goal of knowing Christ? When in the past month have you felt the supernatural joy of Christ?

March 6

The Almighty is beyond our reach and exalted in power; in his justice and great righteousness, he does not oppress.

Job 37:23

Why is it hard not to "get back" at your spouse in small ways when he or she has hurt you?

October 27

Do nothing out of selfish ambition or vain conceit, but in humility consider others better than yourselves. Each of you should look not only to your own interests, but also to the interests of others.

Philippians 2:3-4

Name a couple of your mate's quirks that are actually expressions of his or her love for you. Which of your own quirks does your spouse find irritating? How can you use these to express love in a way your spouse understands?

March 7

*It is mine to avenge; I will repay. In due time their foot will slip;
their day of disaster is near and their doom rushes upon them.*

Deuteronomy 32:35

How can you trust God to handle the situation
when others wrong you?

October 26

And this is my prayer: that your love may abound more and more in knowledge and depth of insight, so that you may be able to discern what is best and may be pure and blameless until the day of Christ, filled with the fruit of righteousness that comes through Jesus Christ—to the glory and praise of God.

Philippians 1:9-11

What are some of your hopes or goals for your future spiritual development?

March 8

*My ears had heard of you but now
my eyes have seen you.*

Job 42:5

When has a period of instability been uncomfortable?
When has change been an opportunity for growth?

October 25

Being confident of this, that he who began a good work in you will carry it on to completion until the day of Christ Jesus.

Philippians 1:6

In what specific areas have you grown in your understanding of God and in your life as a Christian?

March 9

But his delight is in the law of the LORD,
and on his law he meditates day and night.

Psalm 1:2

How do you manage to reflect on what you've learned from
Scripture when you're constantly battling distractions?

October 24

Submit to one another out of reverence for Christ.
Ephesians 5:21

What can the two of you do in the days ahead to show your
respect for each other? Use a comprehensive concordance
to explore the "one another" commands of the New Testament.
Which of these would most enrich your marriage?

March 10

How sweet are your words to my taste,
sweeter than honey to my mouth!

Psalm 119:103

What is something you've recently learned from God's Word that
you might share with your spouse this week?

October 23

A gentle answer turns away wrath, but a harsh word stirs up anger.

Proverbs 15:1

What's the best way you have found for communicating
your forgiveness after a disagreement?

March 11

I will lie down and sleep in peace, for you alone, O LORD, make me dwell in safety.

Psalm 4:8

Is there an area or issue in your life in which you need to experience God's rest and peace? When have you felt a God-given rest or peace after particularly difficult times?

October 22

*"In your anger do not sin": Do not let the sun
go down while you are still angry.*

Ephesians 4:26

Take a minute to remember and assess your own
patterns of behavior when you are angry. Do you tend to
assign blame, or strike back with icy silence?

March 12

*They cried to you and were saved; in you they trusted
and were not disappointed.*

Psalm 22:5

How does your "ultimate hope" carry you in times
of disappointment or discouragement?

October 21

*Now to him who is able to do immeasurably more than
all we ask or imagine, according to his power that is at work within us,
to him be glory in the church and in Christ Jesus throughout all
generations, for ever and ever! Amen.*

Ephesians 3:20-21

What do you most enjoy about being married?
Which activities could help the two of you celebrate
the joy and the fun of your life together?

March 13

For he has not despised or disdained the suffering of the afflicted one;
he has not hidden his face from him but has listened to his cry for help.

Psalm 22:24

How does having two of you to cope with troubles
give you courage as you face the future?

October 20

For we are God's workmanship, created in Christ Jesus to do
good works, which God prepared in advance for us to do.
Ephesians 2:10

When have you seen that God prepared you in your past to deal
with some challenge in your present experience? How can you have
assurance that God will meet your needs in the future?

March 14

Guide me in your truth and teach me, for you are God my Savior,
and my hope is in you all day long.

Psalm 25:5

What are some favorite Scripture passages that you
find yourself returning to over and over? What personal
needs do they address for you?

October 19

*He predestined us to be adopted as his sons through Jesus Christ,
in accordance with his pleasure and will.*

Ephesians 1:5

Have the two of you ever attempted something
"risky" because you believed God was leading you?
What was the outcome of that venture?

March 15

*For his anger lasts only a moment, but his favor lasts a lifetime;
weeping may remain for a night, but rejoicing comes in the morning.*

Psalm 30:5

Have you ever known a person whose anger was his
or her defining characteristic? How was that person's
anger a handicap to him or her?

October 18

Brothers, if someone is caught in a sin, you who are spiritual should restore him gently. But watch yourself, or you also may be tempted.
Galatians 6:1

What are some outside problems or stresses that might be putting strains on your marital relationship? How do you think the two of you could defuse some of those issues or offset the stressful times?

March 16

*Be kind and compassionate to one another, forgiving each other,
just as in Christ God forgave you.*

Ephesians 4:32

What difference would "quick" forgiveness make in
the atmosphere of your home?

October 17

Since we live by the Spirit, let us keep in step with the Spirit. Let us not become conceited, provoking and envying each other.

Galatians 5:25-26

In what areas can you see that the indwelling Holy Spirit has born "fruit" in the way you treat your spouse?

March 17

You have made my days a mere handbreadth; the span of my years is as nothing before you. Each man's life is but a breath.

Psalm 39:5

When can you set aside a time this week to sit down with your spouse for talk and reflection? What topics would you like to discuss when you are together?

October 16

*But the fruit of the Spirit is love, joy, peace, patience,
kindness, goodness, faithfulness, gentleness and self-control.
Against such things there is no law.*

Galatians 5:22-23

Privately consider ways you might evidence kindness
and gentleness toward your spouse today.

March 18

Be still, and know that I am God; I will be exalted among the nations, I will be exalted in the earth.

Psalm 46:10

`Have you ever felt that your marriage should be better faster? Why is it hard to be patient as relationships develop?

October 15

*That is why, for Christ's sake, I delight in weaknesses,
in insults, in hardships, in persecutions, in difficulties.
For when I am weak, then I am strong.*

2 Corinthians 12:10

How can you be strong when you are weak?

March 19

Restore to me the joy of your salvation and grant me
a willing spirit, to sustain me.

Psalm 51:12

When has constant busyness sapped your joy as a
Christian? How did you respond? What activities refresh
you rather than fatigue you?

October 14

But he said to me, "My grace is sufficient for you, for my power is made perfect in weakness." Therefore I will boast all the more gladly about my weaknesses, so that Christ's power may rest on me.

2 Corinthians 12:9

What unrealistic expectations might
you have about your spouse?

March 20

I said, "Oh, that I had the wings of a dove!
I would fly away and be at rest—
. . . I would hurry to my place of shelter,
far from the tempest and storm."

Psalm 55:6,8

What is the best balance for you for time together and time apart?

October 13

Now he who supplies seed to the sower and bread for food will also supply and increase your store of seed and will enlarge the harvest of your righteousness.

2 Corinthians 9:10

How can the two of you make sure that giving is a source of satisfaction and joy and not just an obligation or difficulty?

March 21

But Jesus often withdrew to lonely places and prayed.
Luke 5:16

What are two times this week when you can offer your
spouse the gift of solitude?

October 12

Remember this: Whoever sows sparingly will also reap sparingly,
and whoever sows generously will also reap generously. Each man
should give what he has decided in his heart to give, not reluctantly or
under compulsion, for God loves a cheerful giver.

2 Corinthians 9:6-7

How does giving benefit you?

March 22

My soul finds rest in God alone; my salvation comes from him.
Psalm 62:1

How does the prospect of change affect you? Think of one time when change was difficult for you. How did your spouse and your faith help you deal with that change?

October 11

Therefore, if anyone is in Christ, he is a new creation;
the old has gone, the new has come!
2 Corinthians 5:17

How do you feel about having someone else get so close to the real you? How can the intimate knowledge of each other that you share as married Christians be an important asset to personal growth?

March 23

*Praise be to God, who has not rejected my prayer
or withheld his love from me!*

Psalm 66:20

How does self-sufficiency have a damaging effect
on an effective prayer life?

October 10

We are hard pressed on every side, but not crushed; perplexed, but not in despair; persecuted, but not abandoned; struck down, but not destroyed. We always carry around in our body the death of Jesus, so that the life of Jesus may also be revealed in our body.

2 Corinthians 4:8-10

What things are you struggling with—as individuals, as a couple, as a family? Remember God's promise of "an eternal glory that far outweighs them all."

March 24

If I had cherished sin in my heart, the Lord would not have listened.
Psalm 66:18

What role does confession of sin play in your
times of shared prayer?

October 9

*For our light and momentary troubles are achieving for us
an eternal glory that far outweighs them all.*

2 Corinthians 4:17

What do you most look forward to about heaven?

March 25

God sets the lonely in families, he leads forth the prisoners with singing;
but the rebellious live in a sun-scorched land.

Psalm 68:6

Have you ever found yourself in a position of leading or teaching
someone else's child? What were the drawbacks—and rewards?

October 8

And we, who with unveiled faces all reflect the Lord's glory,
are being transformed into his likeness with ever-increasing glory,
which comes from the Lord, who is the Spirit.

2 Corinthians 3:18

It's clear that God wants to help people change for the better. Why
do you think change is so difficult in a marriage relationship? Why is
it so hard to help each other change? How can God help?

March 26

He upholds the cause of the oppressed and gives food to the hungry. The LORD sets prisoners free, the LORD gives sight to the blind, the LORD lifts up those who are bowed down, the LORD loves the righteous.

Psalm 146:7-8

What ministry could a family have just through their life together as Christians?

October 7

*For no matter how many promises God has made,
they are "Yes" in Christ. And so through him the "Amen"
is spoken by us to the glory of God.*

2 Corinthians 1:20

What life experiences have forced you to trust
God more completely? What role did prayer play as
you went through those times? How does meeting God
"face-to-face" build your trust in him?

March 27

For zeal for your house consumes me, and the insults of those who insult you fall on me.

Psalm 69:9

What would it take for your angry times to be productive times for your relationship? Remember the last time the two of you expressed your anger to one another. Was it constructive? Why or why not?

October 6

Love is patient, love is kind. It does not envy, it does not boast, it is not proud. It is not rude, it is not self-seeking, it is not easily angered, it keeps no record of wrongs.

1 Corinthians 13:4-5

How can you improve your communication radar when it comes to listening to your spouse?

March 28

Better is one day in your courts than a thousand elsewhere;
I would rather be a doorkeeper in the house of my God than dwell
in the tents of the wicked.

Psalm 84:10

For what things in your marriage are you thankful on a
day-to-day basis? When you realize you're "terminal"—that at any
time you might be in heaven with God—how does it affect the
decisions you make in your marriage and family?

October 5

Love does not delight in evil but rejoices with the truth. It always protects, always trusts, always hopes, always perseveres. Love never fails.

1 Corinthians 13:6-8a

What benefits and pitfalls come with the familiarity
of having been married for years?

March 29

He will not always accuse, nor will he harbor his anger forever; he does not treat us as our sins deserve or repay us according to our iniquities.

Psalm 103:9-10

In what ways have you rebelled against God in the past?

October 4

There are different kinds of gifts, but the same Spirit. There are different kinds of service, but the same Lord. There are different kinds of working, but the same God works all of them in all men.

1 Corinthians 12:4-6

List five differences between you and your spouse in personality, outlook and daily routine. How do these differences make your marriage more balanced and complete?

March 30

As a father has compassion on his children, so the LORD has compassion on those who fear him.

Psalm 103:13

In what ways have your children rebelled against you?
How have you handled the problem?

October 3

Follow my example, as I follow the example of Christ.
1 Corinthians 11:1

What words do you think your spouse would use to describe the positive qualities you teach by example? What other traits would you like your children to remember?

March 31

*Let them give thanks to the LORD for his unfailing love and
his wonderful deeds for men, for he satisfies the thirsty and fills
the hungry with good things.*

Psalm 107:8-9

How does gratitude free you from anxiety over what you don't have?
How can giving up those false expectations actually help you meet
each other's needs even better in the future?

October 2

So whether you eat or drink or whatever you do,
do it all for the glory of God.

1 Corinthians 10:31

How can you be more sensitive to the little
things your spouse may need?

April 1

This is the day the LORD has made;
let us rejoice and be glad in it.
Psalm 118:24

What are the everyday things you love about home and your life
together? What things about today can you "be joyful" about?

October 1

Nobody should seek his own good, but the good of others.
1 Corinthians 10:24

What sensitivities does your spouse show that
you are especially thankful for?

April 2

Sons are a heritage from the LORD,
children a reward from him.

Psalm 127:3

What are some of the "cheap substitutes" young people
turn to instead of turning to their parents? Brainstorm
ways you might communicate attitudes of love and
acceptance toward your children.

September 30

*The man who thinks he knows something does not yet know as he ought
to know. But the man who loves God is known by God.*

1 Corinthians 8:2-3

What are some of the most positive things you
experienced or learned while you were growing up that you'd
like your children to learn from, too?

April 3

Your kingdom is an everlasting kingdom, and your dominion endures through all generations. The LORD is faithful to all his promises and loving toward all he has made. The LORD upholds all those who fall and lifts up all who are bowed down.

Psalm 145:13-14

Why do you think the myth that busyness is always good is so pervasive?

September 29

We know that we all possess knowledge.
Knowledge puffs up, but love builds up.
1 Corinthians 8:1b

In what ways do you see your kids struggling with some
of the same problems you had as a child?

April 4

A generous man will prosper; he who refreshes others will himself be refreshed.

Proverbs 11:25

How do you and your spouse provide "breathing" time for each other?

September 28

*Each man has his own gift from God; one has this gift,
another has that. Now to the unmarried and the widows I say: It is
good for them to stay unmarried, as I am. But if they cannot control
themselves, they should marry, for it is better to marry than to
burn with passion. To the married I give this command (not I,
but the Lord): A wife must not separate from her husband.*

1 Corinthians 7:7b-10

Why is it so often ineffective to try to "change" your spouse?
As you hope for continual improvement in your relationship,
how can you trust God for the future?

April 5

My son, if you accept my words and store up my commands within you, turning your ear to wisdom and applying your heart to understanding, . . . then you will understand the fear of the LORD and find the knowledge of God.

Proverbs 2:1–2,5

In your life, who have been your models for godliness and service? What specific attitudes or actions impressed you?

September 27

The wife's body does not belong to her alone but also to her husband. In the same way, the husband's body does not belong to him alone but also to his wife.

1 Corinthians 7:4

Over the past years of your marriage, what were some of the "marital realities" that have been accepted or overlooked because of grace? Why does it take grace to receive love and kindness as well as to give it?

April 6

He holds victory in store for the upright, he is a shield to those whose walk is blameless, for he guards the course of the just and protects the way of his faithful ones.

Proverbs 2:7-8

What godly attitudes and behaviors have you seen in your spouse? How have you been able to incorporate some of them into your own life?

September 26

Do you not know that your body is a temple of the Holy Spirit, who is in you, whom you have received from God? You are not your own; you were bought at a price. Therefore honor God with your body.

1 Corinthians 6:19-20

What attitudes and actions should you avoid because they would threaten the exclusivity and permanence of your marriage?

April 7

Let love and faithfulness never leave you; bind them around your neck, write them on the tablet of your heart. Then you will win favor and a good name in the sight of God and man.

Proverbs 3:3-4

What difficult circumstances are you facing that require you to choose to be faithful? How can you demonstrate love and faithfulness to your spouse in new ways this week?

September 25

Flee from sexual immorality. All other sins a man commits are outside his body, but he who sins sexually sins against his own body.

1 Corinthians 6:18

What led you to commit yourself in marriage to your spouse?

April 8

Wisdom is supreme; therefore get wisdom.
Though it cost all you have, get understanding.

Proverbs 4:7

What have you learned about your spouse that you
picked up just by watching him or her? How could you be
a better observer of your spouse?

September 24

But God chose the foolish things of the world to shame the wise;
God chose the weak things of the world to shame the strong.
1 Corinthians 1:27

What are some of the simple things about
married life that bring you joy? How do your actions
show the love of God to your spouse?

April 9

*May your fountain be blessed, and may you rejoice
in the wife of your youth.*

Proverbs 5:18

What are some ways you've found to create "marriage time,"
apart from "family time"? What are some shared interests
you might develop further?

September 23

*I appeal to you, brothers, in the name of our Lord Jesus Christ,
that all of you agree with one another so that there may be no divisions
among you and that you may be perfectly united in mind and thought.*

1 Corinthians 1:10

What strengths do you admire most in your
husband or wife? How have those qualities contributed
to strengthening you as a team?

April 10

A kindhearted woman gains respect,
but ruthless men gain only wealth.

Proverbs 11:16

How does your respect for your spouse encourage him
or her to make the most of talents and gifts? How has your
spouse's respect encouraged you?

September 22

Therefore you do not lack any spiritual gift as you eagerly wait for our Lord Jesus Christ to be revealed. He will keep you strong to the end, so that you will be blameless on the day of our Lord Jesus Christ.

1 Corinthians 1:7-8

If you have ever fallen into the trap of trying to change your spouse, what was the outcome?

April 11

*A wife of noble character is her husband's crown,
but a disgraceful wife is like decay in his bones.*

Proverbs 12:4

When, in the course of your marriage, has your spouse
looked beyond your flaws and conveyed God's unconditional love?
How did it make you feel?

September 21

May the God who gives endurance and encouragement give you a spirit of unity among yourselves as you follow Christ Jesus, so that with one heart and mouth you may glorify the God and Father of our Lord Jesus Christ.

Romans 15:5-6

What are the ways your approach to spiritual things is different from your spouse's? How can those differences be positive for developing a spiritual friendship between the two of you?

April 12

In the Lord, however, woman is not independent of man, nor is man independent of woman. For as woman came from man, so also man is born of woman. But everything comes from God.

1 Corinthians 11:11-12

How could you help develop a climate of unconditional acceptance in your marriage?

September 20

Accept him whose faith is weak, without passing judgment on disputable matters.

Romans 14:1

As you turn your attention to your own spiritual life, what is one area in which you'd like to see growth? Can you think of a concrete way your spouse could encourage you as you grow in that area?

April 13

Plans fail for lack of counsel, but with many advisers they succeed.
Proverbs 15:22

How have research and seeking the counsel of others
played a role in your decisions?

September 19

Rather clothe yourselves with the Lord Jesus Christ,
and do not think about how to gratify the desires of the sinful nature.
Romans 13:14

What do you think is "fair" behavior when you are disagreeing?

April 14

Reflect on what I am saying, for the Lord will give you insight into all this.

2 Timothy 2:7

How does staying in close relationship to God help you when you are faced with a major decision?

September 18

Love does no harm to its neighbor.
Therefore love is the fulfillment of the law.
Romans 13:10

What do you think is a "fair" balance of closeness
and separateness in your marriage?

April 15

A cheerful heart is good medicine, but a crushed spirit dries up the bones.
Proverbs 17:22

How long has it been since you did something together
solely for enjoyment, with no other objectives? Are you
and your mate having enough fun together? If not, what
can you do this month to enjoy each other more?

September 17

Neither height nor depth, nor anything else in all creation, will be able to separate us from the love of God that is in Christ Jesus our Lord.

Romans 8:39

When have you felt spiritually dry? When have you felt like a failure? How does receiving God's enduring love encourage you in times of staleness or spiritual disappointment?

April 16

He who finds a wife finds what is good and receives favor from the LORD.
Proverbs 18:22

What are the different ways the two of you express problems or feelings? Over the years of your marriage, how have you come to understand each other's communication style better?

September 16

Blessed are they whose transgressions are forgiven, whose sins are covered.
Blessed is the man whose sin the Lord will never count against him.

Romans 4:7-8

Privately recall some of your spouse's most irksome habits.
Be honest with yourself: Are these things you should try
not to resent but just put up with? What trivial things about
yourself are you glad your spouse puts up with?

April 17

Train a child in the way he should go, and when he is old he will not turn from it.

Proverbs 22:6

Parents commonly experience guilt when it comes to their kids. What aspects of child-rearing do you and your spouse tend to worry about?

September 15

Therefore no one will be declared righteous in his sight by observing the law; rather, through the law we become conscious of sin.

Romans 3:20

One of God's boundaries for marriage is sexual fidelity and purity. How does that "limit" actually protect you and your marriage? What other ways have you experienced freedom as a result of limits or restraints?

April 18

For we will all stand before God's judgment seat. It is written:
"'As surely as I live,' says the Lord, 'every knee will bow before me;
every tongue will confess to God.'" So then, each of us
will give an account of himself to God.

Romans 14:10b-12

Ultimately, what things are you responsible for as
parents and what choices will be the responsibility of your
children as individuals?

September 14

*Blessed is the man who perseveres under trial, because
when he has stood the test, he will receive the crown of life that
God has promised to those who love him.*

James 1:12

When in the past week have you found spare moments
for "togetherness time"?

April 19

A word aptly spoken is like apples of gold in settings of silver.
Proverbs 25:11

Who is the best listener you know?
What is that person doing that works?

September 13

To those who by persistence in doing good seek glory, honor and immortality, he will give eternal life.

Romans 2:7

How would you rate your marital satisfaction right now?
Is it higher or lower than you expected at this time in your lives?

April 20

*Through patience a ruler can be persuaded,
and a gentle tongue can break a bone.*

Proverbs 25:15

How could you be more open and willing to receiving
helpful criticism from your spouse?

September 12

He traveled through that area, speaking many words of encouragement to the people, and finally arrived in Greece.

Acts 20:2

What do you think is a good balance for what to share and what not to share about work? What is the danger of looking to work successes as a gauge for your self-esteem?

April 21

As iron sharpens iron, so one man sharpens another.

Proverbs 27:17

What first attracted you to your spouse? How has your spouse's spiritual growth contributed to your own?

September 11

Let the word of Christ dwell in you richly as you teach and admonish one another with all wisdom, and as you sing psalms, hymns and spiritual songs with gratitude in your hearts to God. And whatever you do, whether in word or deed, do it all in the name of the Lord Jesus, giving thanks to God the Father through him.

Colossians 3:16-17

What creative techniques could you implement to bring more Scripture into your day (reading a few verses over dinner or just before you go to sleep; Scripture card on your desk or the refrigerator door)?

April 22

*A fool gives full vent to his anger, but a wise man
keeps himself under control.*

Proverbs 29:11

How do you and your spouse come to an agreement about
when it's time to talk about a problem? How could you incorporate
these ground rules as you seek solutions to your disagreements?

September 10

*Now the Bereans were of more noble character than the Thessalonians,
for they received the message with great eagerness and examined the
Scriptures every day to see if what Paul said was true.*

Acts 17:11

How does your decision-making process depend on God's Word?

April 23

*Under three things the earth trembles, under four it cannot
bear up: . . . an unloved woman who is married, and a
maidservant who displaces her mistress.*

Proverbs 30:21,23

Are you a person who lets things pile up until there's an avalanche
of emotions? What about your spouse? What time of day would be
best for a "daily debriefing" between you and your mate?

September 9

If it is serving, let him serve; if it is teaching, let him teach; if it is encouraging, let him encourage; if it is contributing to the needs of others, let him give generously; if it is leadership, let him govern diligently; if it is showing mercy, let him do it cheerfully.

Romans 12:7-8

What are some things you love about your spouse's character?

April 24

She brings him good, not harm, all the days of her life.

Proverbs 31:12

What makes it impossible for spouses always
to "look good" to one another?

September 8

Judas and Silas, who themselves were prophets, said much to encourage and strengthen the brothers.

Acts 15:32

Identify—and mention—some things your spouse *does* that you especially appreciate.

April 25

*Charm is deceptive, and beauty is fleeting; but a woman
who fears the L*ORD *is to be praised.*

Proverbs 31:30

How can you come together in depending on God
to bring "goodness" into your relationship?

September 7

In Joppa there was a disciple named Tabitha (which, when translated, is Dorcas), who was always doing good and helping the poor.

Acts 9:36

Obviously, a spouse is more than a friend. But what characteristics make your spouse a good friend to you? How can you and your spouse prevent loneliness from creeping into your marriage?

April 26

I saw that wisdom is better than folly, just as light is better than darkness.
Ecclesiastes 2:13

What are the things that discourage you? How does the discouragement affect your marriage? How can Christians live with confidence, despite disheartening trends?

September 6

"Salvation is found in no one else, for there is no other name under heaven given to men by which we must be saved." When they saw the courage of Peter and John and realized that they were unschooled, ordinary men, they were astonished and they took note that these men had been with Jesus.

Acts 4:12-13

Think over the past few years. Name one or two
risks you have taken. What type of personal growth
resulted from having taken those risks?

April 27

Two are better than one, because they have a good return for their work:
If one falls down, his friend can help him up. But pity the man
who falls and has no one to help him up!

Ecclesiastes 4:9-10

Describe a time when you were struggling and
your spouse was there for you.

September 5

I will sing of the LORD's great love forever; with my mouth I will make your faithfulness know through all generations.

Psalm 89:1

As parents, what hopes do you have for your children, based on God's promises?

April 28

Though one may be overpowered, two can defend themselves.
A cord of three strands is not quickly broken.

Ecclesiastes 4:12

What are some of the strengths that make the two
of you a good team?

September 4

The promise is for you and your children and for all who are far off—
for all whom the Lord our God will call.

Acts 2:39

How have you seen blessings in your family that
extend to your generation?

April 29

Do not say, "Why were the old days better than these?"
For it is not wise to ask such questions.

Ecclesiastes 7:10

As you look back on your courtship and the early years of
your marriage, what were some of the highlights? What are
some highlights of your marriage today?

September 3

You have made known to me the paths of life; you will
fill me with joy in your presence.

Acts 2:28

What were some of the most enjoyable aspects of
your courtship? How could some of those "dating" behaviors
fit back into your life together today?

April 30

*When times are good, be happy; but when times are bad, consider:
God has made the one as well as the other.*

Ecclesiastes 7:14

Why is it helpful to look at the present
and the future in positive terms?

September 2

They all joined together constantly in prayer, along with the women and Mary the mother of Jesus, and with his brothers.

Acts 1:14

Make a list of things you'd like to pray about together. Consider your family, friends, church, national leaders, world events, specific needs, etc. Break your list into several smaller lists, and try using one list each day for a short time of joint prayer.

May 1

*The quiet words of the wise are more to be heeded than
the shouts of a ruler of fools.*

Ecclesiastes 9:17

What are some of the "better" and "worse" things the two
of you have encountered in your marriage? How has your
spouse helped you improve as a person?

September 1

Now remain in my love. If you obey my commands, you will remain in my love, just as I have obeyed my Father's commands and remain in his love. I have told you this so that my joy may be in you and that your joy may be complete.

John 15:9b-11

How do your children respond when you make time to be together apart from them?

May 2

Words from a wise man's mouth are gracious,
but a fool is consumed by his own lips.

Ecclesiastes 10:12

Do you think married partners should tell each other everything?
What are some things that might be considered off-limits? When
can total honesty be cruel or harmful?

August 31

My command is this: Love each other as I have loved you.

John 15:12

What parenting issues might disappear as
you grow closer as a couple?

May 3

Remember your Creator in the days of your youth, before the days of trouble come and the years approach when you will say, "I find no pleasure in them"— . . . and the dust returns to the ground it came from, and the spirit returns to God who gave it.

Ecclesiastes 12:1,7

What are some of your long-term goals for yourselves, for your marriage, and for your children? What are the things the two of you need to do right away to prepare for possible loss through death?

August 30

*Remain in me, and I will remain in you. No branch can
bear fruit by itself; it must remain in the vine. Neither can you
bear fruit unless you remain in me.*

John 15:4

Which of your current activities seem to take the most "hurry and
effort"? How does your connection to God fit in with those
pressures? From your own experience, what sort of balance between
work and spiritual rest works best for you?

May 4

I belong to my lover, and his desire is for me.
Song of Songs 7:10

How do your expectations about your sexual life seem to be
different from those of your spouse?

August 29

*God is our refuge and strength, an ever-present help in trouble.
Therefore we will not fear, though the earth give way and the
mountains fall into the heart of the sea, though its waters roar and
foam and the mountains quake with their surging.*

Psalm 46:1-3

Identify one or two worrisome areas in your life
now that you need to trustingly release into God's control.

May 5

The husband should fulfill his marital duty to his wife, and likewise the wife to her husband. The wife's body does not belong to her alone but also to her husband. In the same way, the husband's body does not belong to him alone but also to his wife. Do not deprive each other except by mutual consent and for a time, so that you may devote yourselves to prayer.

1 Corinthians 7:3–5a

A senior pastor of one particular church uses eating as a metaphor for sex. Because of busy lifestyles, couples increasingly only have time for that "snack on the run." When was the last time you and your spouse had a "gourmet feast"?

August 28

Peace I leave with you; my peace I give you. I do not give to you as the world gives. Do not let your hearts be troubled and do not be afraid.

John 14:27

When have you been in a situation in which you could trust only God for the outcome?

May 6

Many waters cannot quench love; rivers cannot wash it away.
If one were to give all the wealth of his house for love,
it would be utterly scorned.

Song of Songs 8:7

What do you think is the chief purpose of marriage? When
you come to a period in your marriage that isn't happy or peaceful,
how can you keep alive your commitment to stay together?

August 27

When Jesus saw her weeping, and the Jews who had come along with her also weeping, he was deeply moved in spirit and troubled.

John 11:33

Why is empathy a better way to go when "bearing burdens" with your spouse? When has your spouse's support or fresh perspective been helpful to you in dealing with a work-related problem?

May 7

*Surely God is my salvation; I will trust and not be afraid. The L*ORD*,*
*the L*ORD*, is my strength and my song; he has become my salvation.*

Isaiah 12:2

When have you experienced supernatural joy and peace,
even when surrounded by troubles?

August 26

Love is patient, love is kind. It does not envy,
it does not boast, it is not proud.
1 Corinthians 13:4

How do contentment and acceptance of God's
plan for you help curb destructive comparisons?

May 8

There is no fear in love. But perfect love drives out fear, because fear has to do with punishment. The one who fears is not made perfect in love. We love because he first loved us.

1 John 4:18-19

What things have you been able to share with your spouse simply because you know he or she loves you and is committed to you, no matter what?

August 25

I am not seeking glory for myself; but there is one who seeks it, and he is the judge. . . . If I glorify myself, my glory means nothing. My Father, whom you claim as your God, is the one who glorifies me.

John 8:50,54

How can you keep competition or unhealthy comparisons from creeping into your relationship with each other?

May 9

*Whether you turn to the right or to the left, your ears will hear
a voice behind you saying, "This is the way; walk in it."*
Isaiah 30:21

When have you clearly felt the distinct leading of God?
Was God's leading taking you in a direction you might naturally
have avoided if it were left entirely up to you?

August 24

But God demonstrates his own love for us in this: While we were still sinners, Christ died for us. Since we have now been justified by his blood, how much more shall we be saved from God's wrath through him!

Romans 5:8-9

How has sacrifice been part of love in your marriage relationship?

May 10

How gracious he will be when you cry for help!
As soon as he hears, he will answer you.
Isaiah 30:19b

What important decisions are you facing right now?
What role does joint prayer play in the decision-making process?

August 23

For God so loved the world that he gave his one and only Son, that
whoever believes in him shall not perish but have eternal life.

John 3:16

How does having children of your own affect your perception
of God's sacrifice of his only begotten son?

May 11

*My people will live in peaceful dwelling places, in secure homes,
in undisturbed places of rest.*

Isaiah 32:18

What does your spouse do that makes you feel safe and accepted?

August 22

Jesus said to the servants, "Fill the jars with water"; so they filled them to the brim. . . . And the master of the banquet tasted the water that had been turned into wine. He did not realize where it had come from, though the servants who had drawn the water knew.

John 2:7,9

In what concrete ways is your life more "full" now that you are married? Have there been changes in yourselves or in your relationship that you once would have thought were impossible?

May 12

Carry each other's burdens, and in this way you will fulfill the law of Christ.

Galatians 6:2

If you could change one thing about your home life to make it more of a "safe harbor" for you, what would it be?

August 21

The Word became flesh and made his dwelling among us.
We have seen his glory, the glory of the One and Only, who came
from the Father, full of grace and truth.

John 1:14

When have you experienced a surprising juxtaposition of grace
or peace in the middle of a marital disagreement? What are the
evidences that God is present in your marriage?

May 13

And the glory of the LORD will be revealed, and all mankind together will see it. For the mouth of the LORD has spoken.

Isaiah 40:5

Whose advice do you most value? Why?

August 20

Jesus said, "Father, forgive them, for they do not know what they are doing." And they divided up his clothes by casting lots.

Luke 23:34

What was the cost of God's forgiveness?
What are some of the costs when you forgive others?

May 14

He tends his flock like a shepherd: He gathers
the lambs in his arms and carries them close to his heart;
he gently leads those that have young.

Isaiah 40:11

What are some specific ways you show
your love for your children?

August 19

For the Son of Man came to seek and to save what was lost.
Luke 19:10

As a couple, what are some specific ways your "hands and feet" get "dirty" as you try to reach others with the good news?

May 15

*So do not fear, for I am with you; do not be dismayed,
I am your God. I will strengthen you and help you; I will uphold
you with my righteous right hand.*

Isaiah 41:10

When have you seen God provide for your physical needs
like food and clothing and housing? How did those times serve
to strengthen your faith for the future?

August 18

When Jesus reached the spot, he looked up and said to him, "Zacchaeus, come down immediately. I must stay at your house today." So he came down at once and welcomed him gladly. All the people saw this and began to mutter, "He has gone to be the guest of a 'sinner.'"

Luke 19:5-7

Describe the difference between being *in* the world and being *of* the world.

May 16

When you pass through the waters, I will be with you; and when you pass through the rivers, they will not sweep over you. When you walk through the fire, you will not be burned; the flames will not set you ablaze.

Isaiah 43:2

What kinds of "deep water" or "fire" have you already navigated successfully, with God's help? How was God's presence real and comforting to you in those times?

August 17

At that time Jesus said, "I praise you, Father, Lord of heaven and earth, because you have hidden these things from the wise and learned, and revealed them to little children."

Matthew 11:25

If you are parents, what aspects of parenting do you most enjoy?

May 17

Even to your old age and gray hairs I am he, I am he who will sustain you. I have made you and I will carry you; I will sustain you and I will rescue you.

Isaiah 46:4

What disappointments are you facing as a couple right now?

August 16

But Jesus called the children to him and said,
"Let the little children come to me, and do not hinder them,
for the kingdom of God belongs to such as these."

Luke 18:16

What are some elements of your life that you consider
some of the proofs of God's love for you?

May 18

I am still confident of this: I will see the goodness of the
LORD in the land of the living. Wait for the LORD; be strong
and take heart and wait for the LORD.

Psalm 27:13-14

In the past, when has God brought a "happy ending" to a time
of real struggle and disappointment in your marriage?

August 15

Am I now trying to win the approval of men, or of God?
Or am I trying to please men? If I were still trying to please men,
I would not be a servant of Christ.

Galatians 1:10

What are your personal and shared priorities before the Lord?

May 19

*He was despised and rejected by men, a man of sorrows,
and familiar with suffering. Like one from whom men hide their faces
he was despised, and we esteemed him not.*

Isaiah 53:3

It takes a radical love to serve and support someone who hurts you.
When in your life has someone loved you with that kind of accepting
love? When you are feeling isolated or lonely, how do you
communicate your trouble to your spouse?

August 14

So you also, when you have done everything you were told to do, should say, "We are unworthy servants; we have only done our duty."

Luke 17:10

"Doing our duty" sounds unpleasant. What are the
joys that come along when we do what is right before God?

May 20

All your sons will be taught by the LORD,
and great will be your children's peace.
Isaiah 54:13

How can you help your children avoid mistakes you or your friends
made as teenagers? Anticipate some of the "critical decisions" your
children will encounter during their teen years. How can you help
shape and direct their choices, starting right now?

August 13

*Therefore, since we are surrounded by such a great cloud of witnesses,
let us throw off everything that hinders and the sin that so easily
entangles, and let us run with perseverance the race marked out for us.*

Hebrews 12:1

How does facing the future as a team—and with God's help—
give you courage and confidence?

May 21

The LORD will guide you always; he will satisfy your needs in a sun-scorched land and will strengthen your frame. You will be like a well-watered garden, like a spring whose waters never fail.

Isaiah 58:11

What do you think are your spouse's top three needs? Make a guess, then check with him or her to see if you were right. What practical steps can you take to meet your spouse's most important needs?

August 12

*I will set out and go back to my father and say to him: Father,
I have sinned against heaven and against you. . . . So he got up
and went to his father. But while he was still a long way off, his father saw
him and was filled with compassion for him; he ran to his son,
threw his arms around him and kissed him.*

Luke 15:18,20

What experiences in your marriage have helped teach
you to be supportive of each other?

May 22

Surely the arm of the LORD is not too short to save,
nor his ear too dull to hear.
Isaiah 59:1

What are the clues, verbal or nonverbal, that your spouse gives
that help you know he or she is really hearing what you say?

August 11

Consider the ravens: They do not sow or reap, they have no storeroom or barn; yet God feeds them. And how much more valuable you are than birds!

Luke 12:24

Review your spending during the last week. Do your expenses reflect the attitude that all you have belongs to God? What are other areas you might tend to keep behind a "closed door" instead of letting God have control?

May 23

Therefore, as God's chosen people, holy and dearly loved, clothe yourselves with compassion, kindness, humility, gentleness and patience.

Colossians 3:12

Analyze your own listening style. Do you think your conversational habits are creating an "oasis" for your spouse?

August 10

"Martha, Martha," the Lord answered, "you are worried and upset about many things, but only one thing is needed. Mary has chosen what is better, and it will not be taken away from her."

Luke 10:41-42

What can you do to foster undivided loyalty to Christ, whether in quiet worship or active service?

May 24

*He has sent me to bind up the brokenhearted, to proclaim freedom
for the captives and release from darkness for the prisoners, . . . and
provide for those who grieve in Zion—to bestow on them a crown of beauty
instead of ashes, the oil of gladness instead of mourning, and a
garment of praise instead of a spirit of despair.*

Isaiah 61:1b,3a

When in your life have you most needed the assurance that you
were loved by God? How can you communicate "unconditional love"
to each other on a regular basis?

August 9

But Martha was distracted by all the preparations that had to be made. She came to him and asked, "Lord, don't you care that my sister has left me to do the work by myself? Tell her to help me!"

Luke 10:40

Which comes easier for you, a more contemplative relationship with God (like Mary's) or a more hands-on, active one (like Martha's)?

May 25

*"Your wickedness will punish you; your backsliding
will rebuke you. Consider then and realize how evil and bitter
it is for you when you forsake the LORD your God and have no awe
of me," declares the Lord, the LORD Almighty.*

Jeremiah 2:19

Think back over times when you have forgiven—
and been forgiven by—each other. How did those experiences
strengthen your marriage?

August 8

Jesus said to the woman, "Your faith has saved you; go in peace."
Luke 7:50

What present situations or future risks are facing you now?
Have you trusted them to God?

May 26

"Return, faithless Israel," declares the LORD,
"I will frown on you no longer, for I am merciful,"
declares the LORD, "I will not be angry forever."
Jeremiah 3:12

What might you need to forgive now?

August 7

How can you say to your brother, "Brother, let me take the speck out of your eye," when you yourself fail to see the plank in your own eye? You hypocrite, first take the plank out of your eye, and then you will see clearly to remove the speck from your brother's eye.

Luke 6:42

In your marriage relationship, why is it important to "clear the air" by confessing wrongs and asking for forgiveness?

May 27

Go up and down the streets of Jerusalem, look around and consider, search through her squares. If you can find but one person who deals honestly and seeks the truth, I will forgive this city.

Jeremiah 5:1

Has there ever been a time when it seemed like a lie could make your life a lot simpler? What did you do?

August 6

Do not judge, and you will not be judged. Do not condemn, and you will not be condemned. Forgive, and you will be forgiven.

Luke 6:37

Why is the habit of negative thoughts about others dangerous for you and disappointing to God?

May 28

The LORD detests lying lips,
but he delights in men who are truthful.
Proverbs 12:22

What person in your life is your best
model of honesty or integrity?

August 5

For Christ's love compels us, because we are convinced that one died for all, and therefore all died. And he died for all, that those who live should no longer live for themselves but for him who died for them and was raised again.

2 Corinthians 5:14-15

What responsibilities do you believe come along with being part of God's family?

May 29

*This is what the LORD says: "Stand at the crossroads and look;
ask for the ancient paths, ask where the good way is, and walk in it,
and you will find rest for your souls."*

Jeremiah 6:16a

What are the risks of loving? What makes the
difference between "sticking it out" and staying together
with a better future in mind?

August 4

The Spirit of the Lord is on me, because he has anointed me to preach good news to the poor. He has sent me to proclaim freedom for the prisoners and recovery of sight for the blind, to release the oppressed.

Luke 4:18

Since you became a Christian, what are some ways you've most enjoyed serving God?

May 30

*Heal me, O LORD, and I will be healed; save me and I will be saved,
for you are the one I praise.*

Jeremiah 17:14

What day-to-day annoyances and problems seem trivial when
placed against a backdrop of life and death? How can
you let petty differences and irritations go instead of letting
them cause trouble in your relationship?

August 3

*Blessed is she who has believed that what the Lord
has said to her will be accomplished!*

Luke 1:45

Reflect on a time when you trusted God together
in the midst of diffuclt circumstances. What did you
learn about God's lovingkindness.

May 31

"Can anyone hide in secret places so that I cannot see him?" declares the LORD. *"Do not I fill heaven and earth?"* declares the LORD.

Jeremiah 23:24

Be completely honest with each other: Does either of you feel a lack of acceptance in any area of your marriage? How does your spouse's acceptance of you make it easier for you to become the mate God wants you to be?

August 2

"I am the Lord's servant," Mary answered. "May it be to
me as you have said." Then the angel left her.

Luke 1:38

Do you find it easy or difficult to trust
God with your family's future? What things do you find
it hard to trust to him?

June 1

"For I know the plans I have for you,"
*declares the L*ORD*, "plans to prosper you and not to harm you,*
plans to give you hope and a future."
Jeremiah 29:11

How is waiting a part of lining up your goals
and dreams with what God desires for you?

August 1

Love the Lord your God with all your heart and with all your soul and with all your mind and with all your strength. . . . Love your neighbor as yourself. There is no commandment greater than these.

Mark 12:30-31

What do you think "loving yourself" means?
Why are you responsible to love others, even if your
self-esteem is sometimes low?

June 2

We wait in hope for the LORD; he is our help and our shield. In him our hearts rejoice, for we trust in his holy name. May your unfailing love rest upon us, O LORD, even as we put our hope in you.

Psalm 33:20-22

When was a time when a period of waiting on God was actually productive for you?

July 31

And when you stand praying, if you hold anything against anyone, forgive him, so that your Father in heaven may forgive you your sins.

Mark 11:25

Do you have a tendency to generalize specific things your spouse does wrong into character assassination? How can you separate what he or she *does* from who he or she *is*?

June 3

*Call to me and I will answer you and tell you great and
unsearchable things you do not know.*

Jeremiah 33:3

When have you had to step back from your children's lives and
wait to see how God would work things out? How does knowing that
God is all-knowing and present everywhere comfort you as you
trust each other and your children to his care?

July 30

Whoever wants to become great among you must be your servant, and whoever wants to be first must be slave of all. For even the Son of Man did not come to be served, but to serve, and to give his life as a ransom for many.

Mark 10:43b-45

Do you agree with the statement, "being a spiritual leader is not as much what you *do* as what you *are*"? Why? What are some ways you can provide leadership in your marriage by serving your spouse?

June 4

Because of the LORD's great love we are not consumed, for his compassions never fail. They are new every morning; great is your faithfulness.

Lamentations 3:22-23

Before you were married, what were your expectations of what marriage would be like? How have the realities of marriage ended up showing you God's grace?

July 29

"'If you can'?" said Jesus. "Everything is possible for him who believes."
Mark 9:23

Describe a time when you were amazed at the way God provided
in some difficult, or seemingly impossible, situation. What aspects
of serving the Lord seem frightening or threatening?

June 5

Restore us to yourself, O Lord, that we may return;
renew our days as of old.

Lamentations 5:21

Have you ever experienced a time when you knew
God had forgiven you for something, but felt that others
had not? How do you communicate your forgiveness
and acceptance within your marriage?

July 28

The people ate and were satisfied. Afterward the disciples picked up seven basketfuls of broken pieces that were left over.

Mark 8:8

How have you practiced hospitality in the last month? Have you been generous in ways that required you to trust in God? In God's economy, five loaves of bread and two fish could feed 5,000 people. How have you seen God provide for your family?

June 6

I will give them an undivided heart and put a new spirit in them; I will remove from them their heart of stone and give them a heart of flesh.

Ezekiel 11:19

Why is it helpful to be in fellowship with God before going on to make things right with your spouse?

July 27

And when they found him, they exclaimed: "Everyone is looking for you!" Jesus replied, "Let us go somewhere else—to the nearby villages—so I can preach there also. That is why I have come."

Mark 1:37-38

How satisfied are both of you with your current balance between times of spiritual replenishment and times of outreach?

June 7

But now you must rid yourselves of all such things as these: anger, rage, malice, slander, and filthy language from your lips.

Colossians 3:8

How could a habit of forgiveness between you result in a spirit of freedom and peace in your marriage?

July 26

Very early in the morning, while it was still dark, Jesus got up, left the house and went off to a solitary place, where he prayed.

Mark 1:35

What does it mean to you that Jesus took time out for prayer?

June 8

I will bless them and the places surrounding my hill. I will send down showers in season; there will be showers of blessing.

Ezekiel 34:26

What are some of the blessings God has "showered"
on you and your spouse?

July 25

And surely I am with you always, to the very end of the age.
Matthew 28:20b

What is the power source Christians draw on
as they pursue victory instead of despair?

June 9

*You my sheep, the sheep of my pasture, are people,
and I am your God, declares the Sovereign LORD.*

Ezekiel 34:31

How does a relationship with the Shepherd benefit
your marriage relationship?

July 24

The angel said to the women, "Do not be afraid, for I know that you are looking for Jesus, who was crucified. He is not here; he has risen, just as he said. Come and see the place where he lay."

Matthew 28:5-6

When have you received spiritual encouragement when you were experiencing difficulty or desperation?

June 10

This man Daniel, whom the king called Belteshazzar, was found to have a keen mind and knowledge and understanding, and also the ability to interpret dreams, explain riddles and solve difficult problems. Call for Daniel, and he will tell you what the writing means.

Daniel 5:12

How do each of you communicate during the decision-making process? How could you communicate more effectively with each other when things are bothering you?

July 23

*Going a little farther, he fell with his face to the ground and prayed,
"My Father, if it is possible, may this cup be taken from me.
Yet not as I will, but as you will."*

Matthew 26:39

Have you ever felt God calling you to do something that
you did not feel willing to do? What were the results?
Is there anything you feel God is asking of you as a couple,
but you've been dragging your feet?

June 11

*Now when Daniel learned that the decree had been published,
he went home to his upstairs room where the windows opened toward
Jerusalem. Three times a day he got down on his knees and prayed,
giving thanks to his God, just as he had done before.*

Daniel 6:10

When you take time out of a hectic day to spend time
with God, what things help you to forget your busy
schedule and focus on him?

July 22

So they are no longer two, but one. Therefore what God has joined together, let man not separate.

Matthew 19:6

What were the differences that came as a surprise after you were married? When your differences lead to conflict, how can you reach a positive solution?

June 12

Satisfy us in the morning with your unfailing love,
that we may sing for joy and be glad all our days.

Psalm 90:14

What difference does inner peace make
in the daily pace of your life?

July 21

*In anger his master turned him over to the jailers to be tortured,
until he should pay back all he owed. This is how my heavenly Father will
treat each of you unless you forgive your brother from your heart.*

Matthew 18:34-35

Describe the essential difference between
forgiveness and tolerance.

June 13

*I prayed to the Lord my God . . . "O Lord, the great
and awesome God, who keeps his covenant of love with all
who love him and obey his commands."*

Daniel 9:4

Is one of you more comfortable with
praying out loud than the other?

July 20

Then Peter came to Jesus and asked, "Lord, how many times shall I forgive my brother when he sins against me? Up to seven times?"

Matthew 18:21

What is something you know your spouse has had to forgive you for more than once?

June 14

Now, our God, hear the prayers and petitions of your servant.
For your sake, O Lord, look with favor on your desolate sanctuary.
Daniel 9:17

What topics would you feel most
comfortable praying about together?

July 19

After he had dismissed them, he went up on a mountainside by himself to pray. When evening came, he was there alone.

Matthew 14:23

Why should taking time for yourself be part of the discipline of serving others? Where are some possible "breathing spaces" in your regular workday?

June 15

*Those who are wise will shine like the brightness
of the heavens, and those who lead many to righteousness,
like the stars for ever and ever.*

Daniel 12:3

Where are you in your joint commitment to serve the Lord?
Are there specific areas in which you would like to serve?

July 18

He will not quarrel or cry out; no one will hear his voice in the streets.
A bruised reed he will not break, and a smoldering wick
he will not snuff out, till he leads justice to victory.

Matthew 12:19-20

Why is it helpful to have a sense that how you behave
each moment is important? When have you seen glimpses
of Christ's character in your spouse's behavior?

June 16

*Come, let us return to the LORD. He has torn us to pieces
but he will heal us; he has injured us but he will bind up our wounds.
After two days he will revive us; on the third day he will restore us,
that we may live in his presence.*

Hosea 6:1-2

Think back to a recent disagreement or quarrel. What things
did each of you do to bring the conflict to an end?

July 17

Take my yoke upon you and learn from me, for I am gentle and humble in heart, and you will find rest for your souls.

Matthew 11:29

Jesus says, "learn from me." Can you remember times in Christ's life when he modeled humility? gentleness? servanthood? How is your attitude about the areas in which you are currently serving—at home and at church?

June 17

Let us acknowledge the LORD; let us press on to acknowledge him.
As surely as the sun rises, he will appear; he will come to us like the
winter rains, like the spring rains that water the earth.

Hosea 6:3

How does praying together help you and
your spouse resolve conflict?

July 16

*Every good and perfect gift is from above, coming down from the Father
of the heavenly lights, who does not change like shifting shadows.*

James 1:17

How have you experienced the comfort
of your heavenly Father?

June 18

As a young man marries a maiden, so will your sons marry you; as a bridegroom rejoices over his bride, so will your God rejoice over you.

Isaiah 62:5

What is your favorite story of another couple whose marriage nearly failed but was wonderfully saved? Tell it to your spouse.

July 15

If you, then, though you are evil, know how to give good gifts to your children, how much more will your Father in heaven give good gifts to those who ask him!

Matthew 7:11

What parallels can you draw between your relationship with your children and God's relationship with you?

June 19

I will heal their waywardness and love them freely, for my anger has turned away from them.

Hosea 14:4

What attributes of God made him so passionate and persistent, despite his troubles with his unfaithful Bride—Israel?

July 14

Be careful not to do your "acts of righteousness" before men, to be seen by them. If you do, you will have no reward from your Father in heaven.

Matthew 6:1

What spiritual satisfaction do you feel because God sees your "unrecognized" service toward others?

June 20

And everyone who calls on the name of the LORD will be saved; for on Mount Zion and in Jerusalem there will be deliverance, as the LORD has said, among the survivors whom the LORD calls.

Joel 2:32

How has the divorce of close friends or family members affected your relationship? How can you "call on the name of the LORD" on behalf of your married friends and loved ones?

July 13

But when you give to the needy, do not let your left hand know what your right hand is doing, so that your giving may be in secret. Then your Father, who sees what is done in secret, will reward you.

Matthew 6:3-4

Why is it important to let go of any expectation for reward or recognition from your spouse when you do something kind for him or her?

June 21

Love does not delight in evil but rejoices with the truth.
It always protects, always trusts, always hopes,
always perseveres. Love never fails.
1 Corinthians 13:6-8

Identify a time in your marriage when you did
what was right, even though you didn't *feel* like doing it.
What was the outcome?

July 12

Finally brothers, whatever is true, whatever is noble, whatever is right, whatever is pure, whatever is lovely, whatever is admirable—if anything is excellent or praiseworthy—think about such things.

Philippians 4:8

Talk with your spouse about your times of lovemaking. What would each of you like to be different?

June 22

Do two walk together unless they have agreed to do so?

Amos 3:3

Repeat your wedding promise to your spouse—
with a commitment of "always."

July 11

*But I tell you that anyone who looks at a woman lustfully
has already committed adultery with her in his heart.*

Matthew 5:28

What influences and messages around us promote
unhealthy fantasies?

June 23

*The pride of your heart has deceived you, you who live in the clefts
of the rocks and make your home on the heights, you who say to yourself,
"Who can bring me down to the ground?"*

Obadiah 3

When was the last time you offered to help your mate
rather than choose to get more sleep, invest your time
in a hobby, or stick with your previous plans? What impact
did that decision have on your marriage?

July 10

Blessed are the peacemakers, for they will be called sons of God.
Matthew 5:9

As a couple, what are the troubles you've had that have eventually resulted in greater peace? As you look back over the years of your marriage, what are the things you can call "good"?

June 24

The word of the LORD came to Jonah son of Amittai:
"Go to the great city of Nineveh and preach against it,
because its wickedness has come up before me." But Jonah ran
away from the LORD and headed for Tarshish.

Jonah 1:1-3a

What responsibilities are you carrying that
more rightly belong to God? How can you relax
and trust God in those areas?

July 9

He will turn the hearts of the fathers to their children, and the hearts of the children to their fathers; or else I will come and strike the land with a curse.

Malachi 4:6

When was the last time you had a spontaneous time of love and affection with your kids? How have you seen the need "to be with you" at work in your marriage, as well as in your kids?

June 25

*He has showed you, O man, what is good. And what
does the LORD require of you? To act justly and to love mercy
and to walk humbly with your God.*

Micah 6:8

How does it prove "commitment" for you to *do* what is right, even
when you don't *feel* like it? Why is commitment dynamic (renewed
day by day) instead of static (a one-time promise)?

July 8

I the LORD *do not change. So you,*
O descendants of Jacob, are not destroyed.
Malachi 3:6

How would each of you rate your marriage on the same scale
of one (marginal) to ten (exceptional)? How can communication
ensure that changes in your personalities will promote
growth and togetherness in your relationship?

June 26

Who is a God like you, who pardons sin and forgives the transgression of the remnant of his inheritance? You do not stay angry forever but delight to show mercy.

Micah 7:18

What is the point of speaking the words "I forgive you"?

July 7

Has not the LORD made them one? In flesh and spirit they are his. And why one? Because he was seeking godly offspring. So guard yourself in your spirit, and do not break faith with the wife of your youth. "I hate divorce," says the LORD God of Israel, "and I hate a man's covering himself with violence as well as with his garment," says the LORD Almighty.

Malachi 2:15-16

Why is it impossible to obtain true happiness when you make it your prime goal? How have you worked toward the goal of maturity in your marriage?

June 27

If we confess our sins, he is faithful and just and will forgive us our sins and purify us from all unrighteousness.

1 John 1:9

When have you said, "I forgive you," but then your actions demonstrated you hadn't really forgiven after all?

July 6

In the same way, the Spirit helps us in our weakness. We do not know what we ought to pray for, but the Spirit himself intercedes for us with groans that words cannot express. And he who searches our hearts knows the mind of the Spirit, because the Spirit intercedes for the saints in accordance with God's will.

Romans 8:26-27

Can you make a deal with one another not to blame each other when problems come up but to pray as partners?

June 28

The LORD is good, a refuge in times of trouble.
He cares for those who trust in him.

Nahum 1:7

Why do you think some couples are surprised when troubles come to their marriage? What role does a sense of humor play in handling the common troubles that are part of your married life?

July 5

*So he said to me, "This is the word of the L*ORD *to Zerubbabel:*
*'Not by might nor by power, but by my Spirit,' says the L*ORD *Almighty."*

Zechariah 4:6

You face many challenges in your life together.
How do you face them as partners?

June 29

But the LORD is in his holy temple;
let all the earth be silent before him.
Habakkuk 2:20

What obstacles prevent you from finding
times of quiet before God?

July 4

*"You have planted much, but have harvested little. You eat,
but never have enough. You drink, but never have your fill. You put on
clothes, but are not warm. You earn wages, only to put them in
a purse with holes in it." This is what the LORD Almighty says:
"Give careful thought to your ways."*

Haggai 1:6-7

How does focusing on God's Kingdom contribute to your
marriage relationship? When a dry period comes to your
marriage, how can you consciously put God first?

June 30

There is a time for everything, and a season for every activity under heaven: . . . a time to be silent and a time to speak.

Ecclesiastes 3:1,7b

How could each of you help the other
create personal quiet times?

July 3

The LORD your God is with you, he is mighty to save.
He will take great delight in you, he will quiet you with his love,
he will rejoice over you with singing.

Zephaniah 3:17

How do the nitty-gritty details of life as two married people
sometimes interfere with your desire to be close spiritually? What
are some of the blessings that come because marriage offers a
unique opportunity for spiritual friendship?

July 1

*Seek The LORD, all you humble of the land, you who do
what he commands. Seek righteousness, seek humility; perhaps you
will be sheltered on the day of the LORD'S anger.*

Zephaniah 2:3

Concerning what issues do you currently
feel critical of your spouse?

July 2

Do not judge, or you too will be judged. For in the same way you judge others, you will be judged, and with the measure you use, it will be measured to you.

Matthew 7:1-2

For each area of criticism, can you think of one way that *you* could change to help alleviate the problem?